THE PENGUIN

WINE CELLAR BOOK

WITH AN INTRODUCTION

BY HUON HOOKE

VIKING

Cellaring wine

Cellaring wine is one of life's most rewarding hobbies. Drinking and sharing wine with good friends and good food is one pleasure; storing it and monitoring its maturation is another. There's also the satisfaction of collecting wine. Owning a cellar can give enjoyment, just like owning a fine wristwatch or rare piece of furniture, and maintaining a cellar will deepen your pleasure and understanding of this fascinating product. Wine, after all, is one of few foods that can be aged in the long term, and one of even fewer that improves with time.

Ageing has two important effects on wine: it softens harsh, youthfully unresolved components, such as firm young tannins, and it allows time for the chemical reactions to take place that render wine more complex. These reactions, oxidation and esterification, are at the simplest level the combining of two chemical compounds to form a third — a flavour compound called an ester. When you appreciate that this third compound may itself react with other compounds to form still more new compounds, you can see that the possibilities for complexity of flavour are enormous.

The main reason people cellar wine is to store it for later use. If it improves in the process, then so much the better. Some people keep a cellar simply to store wine bought on one occasion for use over a period of months or years. However most enthusiasts aim to deliberately age their wine in the belief that time will bring about positive changes.

Just how long wine should be cellared and what constitutes improvement is a very subjective matter, and indeed is the cause of much friendly argument. Should a traditional, unwooded, dry Hunter semillon be drunk on release at one year of age or cellared a minimum of five years and up to fifteen? Should a high-alcohol Barossa Valley shiraz be drunk on release at two to three years or kept for a minimum of ten? These are extremes of opinion, and if you quiz wine lovers you'll find a wide spectrum of preferences.

There are no hard-and-fast answers. You may seek the advice of experts and even they are almost certain to differ. In the final analysis, it's your own palate that must be pleased. If you prefer to drink full-bodied, oaky reds young, then drink them young. And don't be browbeaten by other people. The trick is to know your own palate, and to act accordingly.

And a final tip: it's always better to drink a wine a little too young than a little too old. When too young, a wine will probably still give a lot of pleasure; when too old, it will almost certainly disappoint.

Types of cellars

The traditional image of a wine cellar is a dark, dank, mysterious subterranean catacomb filled with rows of dusty bottles, accessed through a trapdoor or perhaps a narrow, candlelit staircase – a treasure-trove filled with ancient bottles that have been transformed magically into ambrosia by the alchemy of time.

In reality, this is a very rare kind of cellar. These days a cellar can be any collection of wine bottles, whether it's just a couple of boxes under the bed or dozens of bottles in a born-again linen press. Most cellars – in Australia at least – are practical and down-to-earth. A basement room, a subfloor space, a large cupboard in the coolest part of the house, an airconditioned above-ground room – these are more likely scenarios.

Underground cellars may be romantic, but many people quickly tire of them. They tend to be inaccessible: moving a carpet and half-tonne sideboard, hoisting a trapdoor, then stumbling down a ladder gets rather tedious after a while! The idea of entering a spider-and-cockroach-infested dungeon also quickly palls. Sure, underground cellars have cool, stable temperatures thanks to the insulating effect of the earth, but depending on where you live, the trade-off is the risk of flooding. This may necessitate a pump and sump

'Let us have wine and women, mirth and laughter,
Sermons and soda-water the day after.'

LORD BYRON, 1788–1824

drainage system, and usually some difficulty of access. (Think about how athletic you'll be in your old age!)

As well, many underground cellars are only partly under-ground and some have a lot of air movement. Others are not especially cool and may still need airconditioning. I also harbour a deep suspicion of the pesticides that have been used over the years – especially under older houses – and the unknown harm they may cause to wine.

CELLARING CONDITIONS

Of profound despair to a wine consultant or auctioneer is to be invited to assess someone's cellar only to find that due to poor storage conditions, much of the wine has gone 'off'. The longer you keep wine, the more important cellaring conditions become. Unfortunately many people start collecting wine without giving much thought to where they're going to keep it and how suitable the conditions are. Sadly, most modern homes have few places for more than several bottles of wine. Not many of us are fortunate enough to live in an old stone house with a capacious basement.

Stability of temperature is just as important as the temperature itself. Too much fluctuation, and the corks can be pushed. Corks lose their elasticity with age, and hence their ability to expand and contract with the glass and the wine. They are easily loosened by temperature variation, and leakers will result. Visible leakage is a danger signal, and such bottles should be consumed forthwith.

'A Book of Verses underneath the Bough,
A Jug of Wine, a Loaf of Bread — and Thou.'

OMAR KHAYYÁM, 1048–1131

A temperature range of anywhere between 10 and 20 degrees Celsius is tolerable, but a consistent temperature higher than 20 degrees Celsius is not advised. European cellars drop as low as 10 degrees Celsius, but this is unnecessarily cold and will slow the rate of wine's development to a snail's pace. For Australian cellars, 16 to 18 degrees Celsius is more practical. Remember that the warmer the mean temperature, the faster your wine will age. If you keep it in a refrigerator it may eventually delight your grandchildren, but is that what you really want? Domestic airconditioners won't drop the temperature below about 16 degrees Celsius so you'll need a much more expensive refrigerated system to get the temperature really cool.

Humidity is the second consideration, and again a range is acceptable. A mean of 70 to 85 per cent is good. If too damp, moulds will form, labels may rot and cartons may collapse; if too dry, corks may dry out and wines may ullage unacceptably. Keep a maximum/minimum thermometer and a hygrometer in your cellar to monitor the climate. If your cellar is very dry, a simple misting system is advisable — but don't wet the cartons!

Store your bottles on their sides — or inverted — to keep the corks wet. Dry corks, especially old ones, lose their ability to maintain an airtight seal.

It hardly seems necessary to state, but heat sources such as hot-water services and ducted-heating systems should always be avoided. Direct sunlight is a no-no; darkness is desirable. Excessive vibration is also to be avoided, as are strong smells such as those from onions, fuel and chemicals, which may be stored in cellars.

When renovating my own house, I deliberately chose to create a new above-ground cellar in the belief that in a hot town like Sydney it would be easier to control the temperature electrically. I also thought a walk-in room dedicated to wine would be more accessible than an underground cellar, which would have been more costly to excavate and waterproof, to say nothing of the hassle of carrying boxes up and down stairs.

My cellar is as simple as they come. It's a rectangular, heavily insulated room with brick external walls, a concrete floor, a solid-timber door and a permanent airconditioner in one wall. It has no windows and none of its walls receives direct sunlight. Inside, the timber floor-to-ceiling racking is designed to hold cases of wine, not single bottles. My theory is that wine is better protected and insulated inside its own box. Even if your room isn't airconditioned, the box will act as a buffer to temperature changes, whereas naked bottles on racks — while they look pretty and are fun to show off — are vulnerable to temperature fluctuation.

The shelving is spaced to take one case of wine per shelf, so I don't have to dig around in stacks of collapsing cardboard boxes to find that elusive bottle. Bottles are easy to find: each box is numbered and its contents listed on a computer file that has a search function. The difficult part is remembering to keep it up-to-date!

THE PITFALLS OF CELLARING

There are many ways to come unstuck when cellaring wine. A friend of mine stored his wine on a concrete floor against a brick wall. Termites, which love cardboard as much as fresh softwood, moved in and quickly made a terrible mess of boxes and labels. While it may be convenient to leave boxes on the floor of your cellar, you do so at your peril.

Excessive humidity will rot your labels and ruin their appearance. Underground cellars can flood, causing untold damage. (Try identifying hundreds of bottles that have lost their labels!) Cockroaches can be a real pest: they're attracted to the glue beneath some labels and will nibble the paper away to get at the glue.

'*Good wine is a good familiar creature if it be well used.*'

WILLIAM SHAKESPEARE, 1564–1616; *Othello*

5

Heat is the most obvious problem. Many people mistakenly assume any underground cellar or subfloor space is going to be ideal, until a hot wind comes roaring through on days of over 40 degrees Celsius and cooks the wine because there's too much air-movement.

And finally, a word of warning. Don't do as I did (and many others, I've since discovered) when they were starting out: don't fill your stash with numbingly tannic, monstrous reds in the mistaken belief that the bigger and tougher the wine the better it will be in time. You'll be disappointed. They'll probably never turn into the nectar you imagined.

How long to cellar wine

This may come as a shock, but most wine is intended and designed to be drunk young; that is, ready to enjoy immediately it's on sale. More than 60 per cent of all Australian wine sold in Australia still comes in a bag-in-box or wine cask, which obviously shouldn't be cellared. Of the bottled wines, only the top-quality wines of certain grape varieties made from grapes grown in certain regions, are recommended for long keeping. Very few dry white wines improve with age. Sparkling wine and tawny port are both matured by the winemaker and released when they're ready to drink. Both can be stored, but very few sparkling wines actually improve or even hold their quality with extended age. Tawny port is matured in the oak and doesn't improve after it's bottled, although it will keep. Vintage port is a different matter: it's designed for cellaring and demands at least ten years – the best ones more like twenty – before it's at its best.

While few dry whites are good keepers, in Australia riesling – especially from the Eden Valley, Clare Valley and Western Australia's Great Southern – is one of two varieties with the most potential. Hunter Valley semillon is the other, although the number of producers of the traditional early-harvested, unwooded, low-alcohol, ageworthy style is relatively small.

Very few Australian pinot noirs keep for more than three or four years and even fewer actually improve beyond their first year or two. The same can be said for rosé and Beaujolais. Cheaper bottled reds don't generally reward

'*Forsake not an old friend; for the new is not comparable to him; a new friend is as new wine; when it is old, thou shalt drink it with pleasure.*'

THE BIBLE, Ecclesiasticus 9:10

> ## '*A meal without wine is like a day without sunshine.*'
>
> LOUIS PASTEUR, 1822–1895

cellaring but usually will keep for five years. On the other hand, most full-bodied reds do keep, and many improve as they age during six to ten years — sometimes longer. We're talking mainly about shiraz and cabernet sauvignon here. Include cabernet merlot and cabernet shiraz blends, but again, do some research to find out whether they're intended to age. Back-labels give some advice, but talking to winemakers or their staff at cellar-door sales, or to a trusted retailer, is the best way to find the answers.

THE WINDOW OF PEAK DRINKABILITY

There's no precise time at which any wine is at its best. Rather, there's a period of years during which it's likely to be at its optimum — and that window of opportunity is different for each style and vintage of wine. A Coonawarra cabernet sauvignon from a good vintage such as 1996 may be pleasant to drink when released at two to three years, but it will improve for probably five or six years. It will plateau for another five or six, then begin a gradual decline which may take another five years until it becomes 'past its best', and maybe another four years until it's deemed to be 'over the hill'. Wines do not suddenly approach and fall over a cliff: they decline gradually, and their maturation curve is speeded or retarded by the temperature of your cellar.

Lesser-quality vintages tend to age quickly and reach their peaks sooner, then hold their peaks for a shorter period before beginning their decline, which, when it comes, is also swifter. Top vintages live longer, age more slowly, reach their peak later and hold it longer. And, of course, the peak will be a higher one. Their window of drinkability is much greater and their decline will be more gradual.

'*O for a beaker full of the warm South, Full of the true, the blushful Hippocrene, With beaded bubbles winking at the brim, And purple-stained mouth.*'

JOHN KEATS, 1795–1821

8

If all this sounds terribly imprecise and quite a lot like guesswork, don't be put off. Even a little experience will teach you a lot about how wine ages, and there's no time to start like the present!

AUSTRALIAN WINES THAT REWARD CELLARING

Happiness is a red under the bed, and there are more cellarable Australian wines available now than ever before. This is contrary to the popular overseas myth that Australia makes good drink-now wines, but few that really keep.

Penfolds Grange is in a league of its own as the most cellarable Australian wine, in terms of both longevity and financial reward. Access Economics has estimated Grange gives a return on investment of about 110 per cent over five years, putting it ahead of bonds, bank bills, coins, stamp errors, taxi plates, Australian art and real estate. There has been a gulf between Grange and the next-best, Henschke Hill of Grace, but lately the latter has been performing at least as well as Grange in the auctions. In terms of potential return on money invested, these are followed by Mount Mary Cabernets, Moss Wood Cabernet Sauvignon, Petaluma Coonawarra, Penfolds Bin 707 Cabernet Sauvignon, Wynns John Riddoch, Yarra Yering Dry Red No. 1, Henschke Mount Edelstone and Cyril Henschke Cabernet, and Brokenwood Graveyard. And, of course, the great vintages of red Bordeaux are amongst the world's best cellaring wines.

But there's a difference between cellaring for investment and cellaring for drinking pleasure. The latter is the only consideration for most wine lovers, and the field is enormous. My recommendations for Australian red wine are Coonawarra (especially cabernet sauvignon and cabernet blends); Margaret River and Mount Barker, Western Australia; the Barossa (especially Penfolds and Henschke); the Yarra Valley; the central Victorian reds of Bendigo, the Pyrenees, Heathcote and Great Western; McLaren Vale; Clare-Watervale; and Hunter shiraz from good red years (especially Brokenwood, Rothbury, Tyrrell's, Lindemans, Thalgara). There are also some great McLaren Vale/ Coonawarra red blends.

Don't overlook white wines, either. There are many that warrant keeping, such as rieslings from the Clare Valley, Eden Valley and Adelaide Hills, the Victorian high country (Knights, Delatite, Brown Brothers Whitlands), southwest Western Australia (Mount Barker, Frankland, the Porongurup Ranges) and Tasmania. Semillons, especially those made from early-picked grapes vinified without oak, by the traditional Hunter Valley makers, are arguably the best cellaring whites in the country. Not many chardonnays age well, but I'd recommend Leeuwin Estate Art Series, Pierro, Cullen, Moss Wood, Petaluma, Coldstream Hills Reserve, Tyrrell's Vat 47, Bannockburn, Mountadam, Katnook and Hardys Eileen Hardy, to name a few.

The cellaring habit

It's fashionable for people in the wine trade to lament the supposed decline in the timeworn ritual of cellaring wine. 'People don't cellar wine any more,' they cry, wringing their hands and dribbling into their chardonnay. 'They have no patience; they don't understand the taste of aged wine' et cetera, et cetera. I've lost count of the number of retailers and vignerons who have told me sagely that 98 per cent of bottled wine is drunk within hours of being purchased, but no one knows who started this widely-quoted 'fact' and all attempts to trace its source have failed.

In truth, there are no statistics on the incidence of cellaring. I suspect that there are just as many people cellaring wine now as there were in 'the good old days' – whenever they were. It's just that because the total wine market has grown so enormously, the proportion of cellarers seems small. Perhaps the cellarers haven't increased at the same pace as the market. This may reflect modern living situations, with more people moving into home units and flats and generally having little storage space.

Many people would like to keep a cellar and allow their wine to mature, but lack the willpower. 'I can't keep my hands off it' is a common complaint. Others are frightened by the idea of starting a cellar because they imagine that they'll need thousands of dollars to invest and that the wine will have to be tied up for fifteen or twenty years. The truth is, the most worthwhile kind

'*Wine is a constant proof that God loves us and likes to see us happy.*'

BENJAMIN FRANKLIN, 1706–1790

9

'Very good in its way
Is the Verzenay,
Or the Sillery soft
and creamy;
But Catawba wine
Has a taste more divine,
More dulcet, delicious
and dreamy.'

HENRY WADSWORTH LONGFELLOW, 1807–1882

of cellaring plan is a short-term one, and you don't need to incarcerate wine for decades before you can reap rewards.

Even short-term cellaring of three to five years can elevate most reds and many whites to a more interesting plane. With today's business pressures – the cost of money, the need for constant cashflow, and so on – wine companies are putting their product on sale earlier than ever. These immature products cry out for cellaring.

Some people would like to cellar wine, but they're worried they won't live long enough to drink it in the glory of its maturity. They should rest assured they don't have to lock it up and throw away the key. A good riesling is usually lovely from the word go, but give it two or three years and you'll see the proverbial multicoloured butterfly emerge from the chrysalis.

Short-term cellaring need not involve young wine. Wines that have very long lifespans, such as the better growths of Bordeaux, Burgundy and the Rhone Valley, and Penfolds Grange, can be bought at auction or from retailers midway through their lives, at say ten years old, then cellared for another five or so. I like to buy these sorts of wines at the start of their drinking window, and cellar them until I find an occasion to open them, which might be anything up to five years later or more.

One of the pleasures to be had from the cellaring habit is realising, some years down the track, that you've made a good buying decision. Occasionally I dig out an old bottle, still with its price-sticker affixed, and after finding it's in excellent drinking order, marvel at the pittance I paid. For instance, a 1979 Bowen Estate Cabernet Sauvignon I recently enjoyed had a Nick's Wine Merchants sticker revealing I'd paid $4.80 for it. That was in 1981 or '82 when $4.80 was a lot for a bottle of wine!

STARTING A CELLAR

So you've got your $2000 tax-refund cheque, you've cleared a space in the garage and you've decided to start a cellar. Where to start? What to buy?

There are many ways the uninitiated can find guidance. Your best bet is to seek out a good merchant. There are more and more retail shops with a good range of wines and knowledgeable staff. Cultivate one of the latter and with luck they'll get to know your tastes.

There are several wine magazines, and many newspapers regularly carry wine articles. Guidebooks are also available. All are well worth consulting.

Talk to the winemakers themselves at exhibitions, public tastings and when touring wineries. Join mailing lists for winery and retailer newsletters. Enrol in a wine appreciation course. And finally, trial and error is the best teacher. Just have a go.

Huon Hooke
March 1999

Huon Hooke is a leading wine writer and wine judge. He is also co-author of the annual Penguin Good Australian Wine Guide.

How to use this book

The Penguin Wine Cellar Book is designed to help you catalogue and keep track of your wine collection. In doing this, it develops progressively into a wine-lover's journal, enticing you to keep a diary of the pleasure you've had drinking the wines you've cellared, sharing them with good friends and good food over the years.

This book is most useful for wines purchased in quantities of at least six bottles, preferably a dozen. Use the two-page grid provided for each wine. There are no rights or wrongs here: write as much or as little as you wish. See the samples in the grid reproduced opposite for ideas on how to begin.

Most of the information 'cells' in the grid are self-explanatory, although 'Cellar location' may need some elucidation. If the wine is stored in a box, it's handy to number or letter each box for easy reference, for example 25, 26; A1, A2, A3, and so on. If the wine is in a rack, a simple cataloguing system can be created by naming each space with a number and a letter. The letters might refer to the horizontal axis, and the numbers to the vertical axis. Hence, C7 would be the third row from the left, and the seventh row down from the top.

If each space is given an identity and all the spaces housing bottles of a particular description are listed under 'Cellar location', each bottle can be located quickly. As you drink a bottle, cross it out. That space then becomes available for another wine to be placed in it and catalogued accordingly.

Remember, wine is made for drinking. Enjoy your cellar, but more importantly, enjoy your wine.

Wine

PRODUCER

Dalwhinnie

VARIETY/BRAND NAME

Moonambel Shiraz

VINTAGE

1990

Qty purchased	Date
12	1/8/1992
From	Price
the winery	$18.00

Cellar location
Box A1; C4, C5, C6, ☒,
☒, ☒, F3, F4

Date	Btls left	Occasion/Company	Food	Comments	Score /10
31/12/1999	7	At home with the family, and Joe and Liz, on New Year's Eve.	Heidi Gruyere cheese.	Starting to show some maturity and great complexity. Rich, full-bodied, smooth, with just a hint of regional peppermint. Superb. (It's now fetching $65 a bottle at auction!)	9.5/10
10/4/2000	6	At Claude's restaurant on Bill's birthday, with the Schmidts, the Johnsons, Joan and Bill.	Beef tournedos with wild mushrooms and red-wine reduction.	Even better than usual: still improving. Stood up very well beside a 1990 Chave Hermitage.	10/10
22/11/2000	5	At the Johnsons' house on Sam's 40th birthday, with Jack and Virginia.	Braised veal shanks.	The dish brought out the best in the wine and vice versa. Velvety, chunky, spices and plums. No hurry to drink the other bottles!	10/10

Wine

PRODUCER

_____

VARIETY/BRAND NAME

_____

VINTAGE

_____

'*Wine cheers the sad, revives the old, inspires the young, makes weariness forget his toil.*'

LORD BYRON, 1788–1824

Qty purchased	Date
From	Price
Cellar location	

DATE	BTLS LEFT	OCCASION/COMPANY

Food	Comments	Score /10

Wine

PRODUCER

VARIETY/BRAND NAME

VINTAGE

Qty purchased	Date
From	Price
Cellar location	

Date	Btls left	Occasion/Company

Wine

PRODUCER

VARIETY/BRAND NAME

VINTAGE

Qty purchased	Date
From	Price

Cellar location

DATE	BTLS LEFT	OCCASION/COMPANY

FOOD	COMMENTS	SCORE /10

Wine

PRODUCER

VARIETY/BRAND NAME

VINTAGE

Qty purchased	Date
From	Price
Cellar location	

DATE	BTLS LEFT	OCCASION/COMPANY

FOOD	COMMENTS	SCORE /10

Wine

PRODUCER

VARIETY/BRAND NAME

VINTAGE

Qty purchased	Date
From	Price

Cellar location

DATE	BTLS LEFT	OCCASION/COMPANY

Wine

PRODUCER

VARIETY/BRAND NAME

VINTAGE

> '*Give me books, fruit, French wine and fine weather and a little music out of doors.*'
>
> JOHN KEATS, 1795–1821

Qty purchased	Date
From	Price
Cellar location	

DATE	BTLS LEFT	OCCASION/COMPANY

Wine

PRODUCER

VARIETY/BRAND NAME

VINTAGE

Qty purchased	Date
From	Price

Cellar location

DATE	BTLS LEFT	OCCASION/COMPANY

FOOD	COMMENTS	SCORE /10

Wine

PRODUCER

VARIETY/BRAND NAME

VINTAGE

Qty purchased	Date
From	Price
Cellar location	

DATE	BTLS LEFT	OCCASION/COMPANY

FOOD	COMMENTS	SCORE /10

Wine

PRODUCER

VARIETY/BRAND NAME

VINTAGE

Qty purchased	Date
From	Price
Cellar location	

DATE	BTLS LEFT	OCCASION/COMPANY

Wine

PRODUCER

VARIETY/BRAND NAME

VINTAGE

Qty purchased	Date
From	Price

Cellar location

DATE	BTLS LEFT	OCCASION/COMPANY

Wine

PRODUCER

VARIETY/BRAND NAME

VINTAGE

'*A bottle of good wine,
like a good act, shines ever
in the retrospect.*'

ROBERT LOUIS STEVENSON, 1850—1894

Qty purchased	Date
From	Price
Cellar location	

DATE	BTLS LEFT	OCCASION/COMPANY

Wine

PRODUCER

VARIETY/BRAND NAME

VINTAGE

Qty purchased	Date
From	Price
Cellar location	

DATE	BTLS LEFT	OCCASION/COMPANY

Wine

PRODUCER

VARIETY/BRAND NAME

VINTAGE

Qty purchased	Date
From	Price

Cellar location

DATE	BTLS LEFT	OCCASION/COMPANY

Wine

PRODUCER

VARIETY/BRAND NAME

VINTAGE

Qty purchased	Date
From	Price
Cellar location	

DATE	BTLS LEFT	OCCASION/COMPANY

Food	Comments	Score /10

Wine

PRODUCER

VARIETY/BRAND NAME

VINTAGE

Qty purchased	Date
From	Price
Cellar location	

DATE	BTLS LEFT	OCCASION/COMPANY

Wine

PRODUCER

VARIETY/BRAND NAME

VINTAGE

*'I love everything that's old:
old friends, old times, old manners,
old books, old wines.'*

OLIVER GOLDSMITH, 1728–1774

Qty purchased	Date
From	Price

Cellar location

DATE	BTLS LEFT	OCCASION/COMPANY

FOOD	COMMENTS	SCORE /10

Wine

PRODUCER

VARIETY/BRAND NAME

VINTAGE

Qty purchased	Date
From	Price
Cellar location	

DATE	BTLS LEFT	OCCASION/COMPANY

FOOD	COMMENTS	SCORE /10

Wine

PRODUCER

VARIETY/BRAND NAME

VINTAGE

Qty purchased	Date
From	Price
Cellar location	

DATE	BTLS LEFT	OCCASION/COMPANY

Wine

PRODUCER

VARIETY/BRAND NAME

VINTAGE

Qty purchased	Date
From	Price
Cellar location	

DATE	BTLS LEFT	OCCASION/COMPANY

Wine

PRODUCER

VARIETY/BRAND NAME

VINTAGE

Qty purchased	*Date*
From	*Price*
Cellar location	

DATE	BTLS LEFT	OCCASION/COMPANY

FOOD	COMMENTS	SCORE /10

# Wine

PRODUCER

VARIETY/BRAND NAME

VINTAGE

'Who loves not wine, woman and song,
Remains a fool his whole life long.'

MARTIN LUTHER, 1483–1546

Qty purchased	Date
From	Price
Cellar location	

DATE	BTLS LEFT	OCCASION/COMPANY

Wine

PRODUCER

VARIETY/BRAND NAME

VINTAGE

Qty purchased	Date
From	Price
Cellar location	

DATE	BTLS LEFT	OCCASION/COMPANY

FOOD	COMMENTS	SCORE /10

Wine

PRODUCER

VARIETY/BRAND NAME

VINTAGE

Qty purchased	Date
From	Price
Cellar location	

DATE	BTLS LEFT	OCCASION/COMPANY

FOOD	COMMENTS	SCORE /10

Wine

PRODUCER

VARIETY/BRAND NAME

VINTAGE

Qty purchased	Date
From	Price

Cellar location

DATE	BTLS LEFT	OCCASION/COMPANY

Wine

PRODUCER

VARIETY/BRAND NAME

VINTAGE

Qty purchased	Date
From	Price
Cellar location	

DATE	BTLS LEFT	OCCASION/COMPANY

Wine

PRODUCER

VARIETY/BRAND NAME

VINTAGE

*'I think wealth has lost much
of its virtue if it has not wine.'*
RALPH WALDO EMERSON, 1803–1882

Qty purchased	Date
From	Price

Cellar location

DATE	BTLS LEFT	OCCASION/COMPANY

FOOD	COMMENTS	SCORE /10

Wine

PRODUCER

VARIETY/BRAND NAME

VINTAGE

Qty purchased	Date
From	Price

Cellar location

DATE	BTLS LEFT	OCCASION/COMPANY

FOOD	COMMENTS	SCORE /10

Wine

PRODUCER

VARIETY/BRAND NAME

VINTAGE

Qty purchased	Date
From	Price

Cellar location

DATE	BTLS LEFT	OCCASION/COMPANY

Wine

PRODUCER

VARIETY/BRAND NAME

VINTAGE

Qty purchased	Date
From	Price
Cellar location	

DATE	BTLS LEFT	OCCASION/COMPANY

Wine

PRODUCER

VARIETY/BRAND NAME

VINTAGE

Qty purchased	Date
From	Price
Cellar location	

DATE	BTLS LEFT	OCCASION/COMPANY

Wine

PRODUCER

VARIETY/BRAND NAME

VINTAGE

'*Wine is a whetstone to wit.*'

BAILEY'S DICTIONARY, 1721

Qty purchased	Date
From	Price

Cellar location

DATE	BTLS LEFT	OCCASION/COMPANY

FOOD	COMMENTS	SCORE /10

Wine

PRODUCER

VARIETY/BRAND NAME

VINTAGE

Qty purchased	Date
From	Price
Cellar location	

DATE	BTLS LEFT	OCCASION/COMPANY

Wine

PRODUCER

VARIETY/BRAND NAME

VINTAGE

Qty purchased	Date
From	Price

Cellar location

Date	Btls left	Occasion/Company

Wine

PRODUCER

VARIETY/BRAND NAME

VINTAGE

Qty purchased	Date
From	Price

Cellar location

DATE	BTLS LEFT	OCCASION/COMPANY

FOOD	COMMENTS	SCORE /10

Wine

PRODUCER

VARIETY/BRAND NAME

VINTAGE

Qty purchased	Date
From	Price

Cellar location

DATE	BTLS LEFT	OCCASION/COMPANY

Wine

PRODUCER

VARIETY/BRAND NAME

VINTAGE

'*Fill ev'ry glass, for wine inspires us,*
And fires us
With courage, love and joy . . .
Is there aught else on earth desirous?'

JOHN GAY, 1685–1732

Qty purchased	Date
From	Price
Cellar location	

DATE	BTLS LEFT	OCCASION/COMPANY

FOOD	COMMENTS	SCORE /10

Wine

PRODUCER

VARIETY/BRAND NAME

VINTAGE

Qty purchased	Date
From	Price
Cellar location	

DATE	BTLS LEFT	OCCASION/COMPANY

Wine

PRODUCER

VARIETY/BRAND NAME

VINTAGE

Qty purchased	Date
From	Price
Cellar location	

DATE	BTLS LEFT	OCCASION/COMPANY

Wine

PRODUCER

VARIETY/BRAND NAME

VINTAGE

Qty purchased	Date
From	Price

Cellar location

DATE	BTLS LEFT	OCCASION/COMPANY

Wine

PRODUCER

VARIETY/BRAND NAME

VINTAGE

Qty purchased	Date
From	Price

Cellar location

DATE	BTLS LEFT	OCCASION/COMPANY

Wine

PRODUCER

VARIETY/BRAND NAME

VINTAGE

'*The Spirit of Wine sang in my glass,*
and I listened with love to his odorous
music, his flushed and magnificent song.'
WILLIAM ERNEST HENLEY, 1849–1903

Qty purchased	Date
From	Price
Cellar location	

DATE	BTLS LEFT	OCCASION/COMPANY

Wine

PRODUCER

VARIETY/BRAND NAME

VINTAGE

Qty purchased	Date
From	Price
Cellar location	

DATE	BTLS LEFT	OCCASION/COMPANY

Wine

PRODUCER

VARIETY/BRAND NAME

VINTAGE

Qty purchased	Date
From	Price
Cellar location	

DATE	BTLS LEFT	OCCASION/COMPANY

Wine

PRODUCER

VARIETY/BRAND NAME

VINTAGE

Qty purchased	Date
From	Price

Cellar location

DATE	BTLS LEFT	OCCASION/COMPANY

FOOD	COMMENTS	SCORE /10

Wine

PRODUCER

VARIETY/BRAND NAME

VINTAGE

Qty purchased	Date
From	Price
Cellar location	

DATE	BTLS LEFT	OCCASION/COMPANY

Wine

PRODUCER

VARIETY/BRAND NAME

VINTAGE

'God in His goodness sent the grapes,
to cheer both great and small;
Little fools will drink too much,
and great fools not at all.'

ANONYMOUS

Qty purchased	Date
From	Price
Cellar location	

DATE	BTLS LEFT	OCCASION/COMPANY

FOOD	COMMENTS	SCORE /10

Wine

PRODUCER

VARIETY/BRAND NAME

VINTAGE

Qty purchased	Date
From	Price
Cellar location	

DATE	BTLS LEFT	OCCASION/COMPANY

Wine

PRODUCER

VARIETY/BRAND NAME

VINTAGE

Qty purchased	Date
From	Price
Cellar location	

DATE	BTLS LEFT	OCCASION/COMPANY

FOOD	COMMENTS	SCORE /10

Wine

PRODUCER

VARIETY/BRAND NAME

VINTAGE

Qty purchased	Date
From	Price
Cellar location	

DATE	BTLS LEFT	OCCASION/COMPANY

FOOD	COMMENTS	SCORE /10

Wine

PRODUCER

VARIETY/BRAND NAME

VINTAGE

Qty purchased	Date
From	Price

Cellar location

DATE	BTLS LEFT	OCCASION/COMPANY

Wine

PRODUCER

VARIETY/BRAND NAME

VINTAGE

'*When the wines were good they pleased my senses, cheered my spirits, improved my moral and intellectual powers, besides enabling me to confer the same benefits on other people.*'
GEORGE SAINTSBURY, 1845–1933

Qty purchased	Date
From	Price
Cellar location	

DATE	BTLS LEFT	OCCASION/COMPANY

FOOD	COMMENTS	SCORE /10

Wine

PRODUCER

VARIETY/BRAND NAME

VINTAGE

Qty purchased	Date
From	Price
Cellar location	

DATE	BTLS LEFT	OCCASION/COMPANY

Food	Comments	Score /10

Wine

PRODUCER

VARIETY/BRAND NAME

VINTAGE

Qty purchased	Date
From	Price
Cellar location	

DATE	BTLS LEFT	OCCASION/COMPANY

Wine

PRODUCER

VARIETY/BRAND NAME

VINTAGE

Qty purchased	Date
From	Price
Cellar location	

DATE	BTLS LEFT	OCCASION/COMPANY

FOOD	COMMENTS	SCORE /10

Wine

PRODUCER

VARIETY/BRAND NAME

VINTAGE

Qty purchased	Date
From	Price
Cellar location	

DATE	BTLS LEFT	OCCASION/COMPANY

FOOD	COMMENTS	SCORE /10

Wine

PRODUCER

VARIETY/BRAND NAME

VINTAGE

'*For when the wine is in,*
the wit is out.'

THOMAS BECON, 1512–1567

Qty purchased	Date
From	Price

Cellar location

DATE	BTLS LEFT	OCCASION/COMPANY

Wine

PRODUCER

VARIETY/BRAND NAME

VINTAGE

Qty purchased	Date
From	Price

Cellar location

DATE	BTLS LEFT	OCCASION/COMPANY

Food	Comments	Score /10

Wine

PRODUCER

VARIETY/BRAND NAME

VINTAGE

Qty purchased	Date
From	Price
Cellar location	

DATE	BTLS LEFT	OCCASION/COMPANY

FOOD	COMMENTS	SCORE /10

Wine

PRODUCER

VARIETY/BRAND NAME

VINTAGE

Qty purchased	Date
.	
From	Price
Cellar location	

DATE	BTLS LEFT	OCCASION/COMPANY

Food	Comments	Score /10

Wine

PRODUCER

VARIETY/BRAND NAME

VINTAGE

Qty purchased	Date
From	Price
Cellar location	

DATE	BTLS LEFT	OCCASION/COMPANY

FOOD	COMMENTS	SCORE /10

Wine

PRODUCER

VARIETY/BRAND NAME

VINTAGE

'Drink no longer water, but use a little wine for thy stomach's sake and thine often infirmities.'

THE BIBLE, Philippians 4:8

Qty purchased	Date
From	Price
Cellar location	

DATE	BTLS LEFT	OCCASION/COMPANY

Wine

PRODUCER

VARIETY/BRAND NAME

VINTAGE

Qty purchased	Date
From	Price

Cellar location

DATE	BTLS LEFT	OCCASION/COMPANY

Wine

PRODUCER

VARIETY/BRAND NAME

VINTAGE

Qty purchased	Date
From	Price

Cellar location

DATE	BTLS LEFT	OCCASION/COMPANY

Wine

PRODUCER

VARIETY/BRAND NAME

VINTAGE

Qty purchased	Date
From	Price

Cellar location

DATE	BTLS LEFT	OCCASION/COMPANY

Wine

PRODUCER

VARIETY/BRAND NAME

VINTAGE

Qty purchased	Date
From	Price

Cellar location

DATE	BTLS LEFT	OCCASION/COMPANY

Wine

PRODUCER

VARIETY/BRAND NAME

VINTAGE

'Wel loved he garleek, oynons, and eek lekes,
And for to drinken strong wyn, reed as blood.'
GEOFFREY CHAUCER, 1340?–1400

Qty purchased	Date
From	Price

Cellar location

DATE	BTLS LEFT	OCCASION/COMPANY

FOOD	COMMENTS	SCORE /10

Wine

PRODUCER

VARIETY/BRAND NAME

VINTAGE

Qty purchased	Date
From	Price
Cellar location	

DATE	BTLS LEFT	OCCASION/COMPANY

FOOD	COMMENTS	SCORE /10

Wine

PRODUCER

VARIETY/BRAND NAME

VINTAGE

Qty purchased	Date
From	Price

Cellar location

DATE	BTLS LEFT	OCCASION/COMPANY

Wine

PRODUCER

VARIETY/BRAND NAME

VINTAGE

Qty purchased	Date
From	Price

Cellar location

DATE	BTLS LEFT	OCCASION/COMPANY

FOOD   COMMENTS   SCORE /10

Wine

PRODUCER

VARIETY/BRAND NAME

VINTAGE

Qty purchased	Date
From	Price

Cellar location

DATE	BTLS LEFT	OCCASION/COMPANY

Wine

PRODUCER

VARIETY/BRAND NAME

VINTAGE

'You'll have no scandal while you dine,
But honest talk and wholesome wine.'

ALFRED, LORD TENNYSON, 1809–1892

Qty purchased	Date
From	Price

Cellar location

DATE	BTLS LEFT	OCCASION/COMPANY

Wine

PRODUCER

VARIETY/BRAND NAME

VINTAGE

Qty purchased	Date
From	Price

Cellar location

DATE	BTLS LEFT	OCCASION/COMPANY

Wine

PRODUCER

VARIETY/BRAND NAME

VINTAGE

Qty purchased	Date
From	Price

Cellar location

DATE	BTLS LEFT	OCCASION/COMPANY

Wine

PRODUCER

VARIETY/BRAND NAME

VINTAGE

Qty purchased	Date
From	Price

Cellar location

DATE	BTLS LEFT	OCCASION/COMPANY

FOOD	COMMENTS	SCORE /10

Wine

PRODUCER

VARIETY/BRAND NAME

VINTAGE

Qty purchased	Date
From	Price
Cellar location	

DATE	BTLS LEFT	OCCASION/COMPANY

FOOD	COMMENTS	SCORE /10

Wine

PRODUCER

VARIETY/BRAND NAME

VINTAGE

'Give me a bowl of wine.
In this I will bury all unkindness.'
WILLIAM SHAKESPEARE, 1564–1616; *Julius Caesar*

Qty purchased	Date
From	Price
Cellar location	

DATE	BTLS LEFT	OCCASION/COMPANY

FOOD	COMMENTS	SCORE /10

Wine

PRODUCER

VARIETY/BRAND NAME

VINTAGE

Qty purchased	Date
From	Price
Cellar location	

DATE	BTLS LEFT	OCCASION/COMPANY

Wine

PRODUCER

VARIETY/BRAND NAME

VINTAGE

Qty purchased	Date
From	Price
Cellar location	

DATE	BTLS LEFT	OCCASION/COMPANY

Wine

PRODUCER

VARIETY/BRAND NAME

VINTAGE

Qty purchased	Date
From	Price
Cellar location	

DATE	BTLS LEFT	OCCASION/COMPANY

Wine

PRODUCER

VARIETY/BRAND NAME

VINTAGE

Qty purchased	Date
From	Price
Cellar location	

DATE	BTLS LEFT	OCCASION/COMPANY

FOOD	COMMENTS	SCORE /10

Wine

PRODUCER

VARIETY/BRAND NAME

VINTAGE

'*All love at first, like generous wine,*
Ferments and frets until 'tis fine.'

SAMUEL BUTLER, 1612–1680

Qty purchased	Date
From	Price

Cellar location

DATE	BTLS LEFT	OCCASION/COMPANY

FOOD	COMMENTS	SCORE /10

Wine

PRODUCER

VARIETY/BRAND NAME

VINTAGE

Qty purchased	Date
From	Price

Cellar location

DATE	BTLS LEFT	OCCASION/COMPANY

FOOD	COMMENTS	SCORE /10

177

Wine

PRODUCER

VARIETY/BRAND NAME

VINTAGE

Qty purchased	Date
From	Price

Cellar location

DATE	BTLS LEFT	OCCASION/COMPANY

FOOD	COMMENTS	SCORE /10

Wine

PRODUCER

VARIETY/BRAND NAME

VINTAGE

Qty purchased	Date
From	Price

Cellar location

DATE	BTLS LEFT	OCCASION/COMPANY

FOOD	COMMENTS	SCORE /10

Wine

PRODUCER

VARIETY/BRAND NAME

VINTAGE

Qty purchased | *Date*

From | *Price*

Cellar location

DATE	BTLS LEFT	OCCASION/COMPANY

Wine

PRODUCER

VARIETY/BRAND NAME

VINTAGE

'*From wine what sudden friendship springs!*'

JOHN GAY, 1685–1732

Qty purchased	Date
From	Price

Cellar location

DATE	BTLS LEFT	OCCASION/COMPANY

Wine

PRODUCER

VARIETY/BRAND NAME

VINTAGE

Qty purchased	Date
From	Price
Cellar location	

DATE	BTLS LEFT	OCCASION/COMPANY

Wine

PRODUCER

VARIETY/BRAND NAME

VINTAGE

Qty purchased	Date
From	Price

Cellar location

DATE	BTLS LEFT	OCCASION/COMPANY

Wine

PRODUCER

VARIETY/BRAND NAME

VINTAGE

Qty purchased	Date
From	Price

Cellar location

DATE	BTLS LEFT	OCCASION/COMPANY

Wine

PRODUCER

VARIETY/BRAND NAME

VINTAGE

Qty purchased	Date
From	Price
Cellar location	

DATE	BTLS LEFT	OCCASION/COMPANY

FOOD   COMMENTS   SCORE /10

Wine

PRODUCER

VARIETY/BRAND NAME

VINTAGE

'One barrel of wine can work more
miracles than a church full of saints.'
OLD ITALIAN PROVERB

Qty purchased	Date
From	Price
Cellar location	

DATE	BTLS LEFT	OCCASION/COMPANY

Wine

PRODUCER

VARIETY/BRAND NAME

VINTAGE

Qty purchased	Date
From	Price
Cellar location	

Date	Btls left	Occasion/Company

Wine

PRODUCER

VARIETY/BRAND NAME

VINTAGE

Qty purchased	Date
From	Price

Cellar location

DATE	BTLS LEFT	OCCASION/COMPANY

FOOD	COMMENTS	SCORE /10

Wine

PRODUCER

VARIETY/BRAND NAME

VINTAGE

Qty purchased	Date
From	Price
Cellar location	

DATE	BTLS LEFT	OCCASION/COMPANY

Wine

PRODUCER

VARIETY/BRAND NAME

VINTAGE

Qty purchased	Date
From	Price
Cellar location	

DATE	BTLS LEFT	OCCASION/COMPANY

FOOD	COMMENTS	SCORE /10

Wine

PRODUCER

VARIETY/BRAND NAME

VINTAGE

'*Wine is the best liquor to wash glasses in.*'
JONATHAN SWIFT, 1667–1745

Qty purchased	Date
From	Price
Cellar location	

DATE	BTLS LEFT	OCCASION/COMPANY

Wine

PRODUCER

VARIETY/BRAND NAME

VINTAGE

Qty purchased	Date
From	Price
Cellar location	

DATE	BTLS LEFT	OCCASION/COMPANY

Wine

PRODUCER

VARIETY/BRAND NAME

VINTAGE

Qty purchased	Date
From	Price

Cellar location

DATE	BTLS LEFT	OCCASION/COMPANY

FOOD	COMMENTS	SCORE /10

Wine

PRODUCER

VARIETY/BRAND NAME

VINTAGE

Qty purchased	Date
From	Price

Cellar location

Date	Btls left	Occasion/Company

Wine

PRODUCER

VARIETY/BRAND NAME

VINTAGE

Qty purchased	Date
From	Price
Cellar location	

DATE	BTLS LEFT	OCCASION/COMPANY

Wine

PRODUCER

VARIETY/BRAND NAME

VINTAGE

'*'Tis pity wine should be so deleterious,*
For tea and coffee leave us much more serious.'

LORD BYRON, 1788–1824

Qty purchased	Date
From	Price
Cellar location	

DATE	BTLS LEFT	OCCASION/COMPANY

Wine

PRODUCER

VARIETY/BRAND NAME

VINTAGE

Qty purchased	Date
From	Price

Cellar location

DATE	BTLS LEFT	OCCASION/COMPANY

Wine

PRODUCER

VARIETY/BRAND NAME

VINTAGE

Qty purchased	Date
From	Price

Cellar location

DATE	BTLS LEFT	OCCASION/COMPANY

Wine

PRODUCER

VARIETY/BRAND NAME

VINTAGE

Qty purchased	Date
From	Price
Cellar location	

DATE	BTLS LEFT	OCCASION/COMPANY

Wine

PRODUCER

VARIETY/BRAND NAME

VINTAGE

Qty purchased	Date
From	Price
Cellar location	

DATE	BTLS LEFT	OCCASION/COMPANY

Wine

PRODUCER

VARIETY/BRAND NAME

VINTAGE

> '*Wine whets the wit, improves its native force*
> *And gives a pleasant flavour to discourse.*'
>
> JOHN POMFRET, 1667–1703

Qty purchased	Date
From	Price
Cellar location	

DATE	BTLS LEFT	OCCASION/COMPANY

Wine

PRODUCER

VARIETY/BRAND NAME

VINTAGE

Qty purchased	Date
From	Price

Cellar location

DATE	BTLS LEFT	OCCASION/COMPANY

FOOD	COMMENTS	SCORE /10

Wine

PRODUCER

VARIETY/BRAND NAME

VINTAGE

Qty purchased	Date
From	Price
Cellar location	

DATE	BTLS LEFT	OCCASION/COMPANY

FOOD	COMMENTS	SCORE /10

Wine

PRODUCER

VARIETY/BRAND NAME

VINTAGE

Qty purchased	Date
From	Price
Cellar location	

DATE	BTLS LEFT	OCCASION/COMPANY

INDEX

To HELP YOU LOCATE your wine entries more easily, fill in the index below. A space is provided for the wine name and its page number. The process of looking up a wine will be even quicker if you keep the wines roughly in alphabetical order.

WINE

PAGE

WINE   PAGE

WINE   PAGE

Viking
Penguin Books Australia Ltd
487 Maroondah Highway, PO Box 257
Ringwood, Victoria 3134, Australia
Penguin Books Ltd
Harmondsworth, Middlesex, England
Penguin Putnam Inc.
375 Hudson Street, New York, New York 10014, USA
Penguin Books Canada Limited
10 Alcorn Avenue, Toronto, Ontario, Canada M4V 3B2
Penguin Books (NZ) Ltd
Cnr Rosedale and Airborne Roads, Albany, Auckland, New Zealand
Penguin Books (South Africa) (Pty) Ltd
5 Watkins Street, Denver Ext 4, 2094, South Africa
Penguin Books India (P) Ltd
11, Community Centre, Panchsheel Park, New Delhi 110 017, India

First published by Penguin Books Australia Ltd 1999

1 3 5 7 9 10 8 6 4 2

Cover design by Guy Mirabella
Text design by Tony Palmer, Penguin Design Studio
Cover illustration by Michelle Katsouranis
Text illustration by Michelle Katsouranis
Typeset in Centaur by Post Pre-press Group, Brisbane
Produced in Australia by the australian book connection

www.penguin.com.au